Effective Internal Auditing

Effective Internal Auditing

Manuel E. Peña-Rodríguez, Esq., PE

Passion for Quality

Business Excellence Consulting, Inc.
PO Box 8326
Bayamón, PR 00960-8326 (USA)
www.bec-global.com
info@bec-global.com

Dedication

To all our customers and readers worldwide.
Your continuous support has enabled us to share with you
our Passion for Quality.

Table of Contents

Preface

Good Manufacturing Practices (GMP) regulations worldwide, as well as the Food and Drug Administration (FDA) and International Conference on Harmonization (ICH) guidances, require that companies have in place an internal quality audit program. For example, the FDA regulation for medical devices establishes that each manufacturer shall establish procedures for quality audits and conduct such audits to assure that the quality system complies with the established quality system requirements, and to determine the effectiveness of the quality system[1]. Also, the ICH Q10 guidance establishes that management should have a formal process for reviewing the pharmaceutical quality system on a periodic basis, which include self-assessment processes, including audits, and external assessments, such as regulatory inspections and findings, and customer audits[2].

Auditing is a powerful management tool in establishing how effectively a company controls the quality of its products and ensures compliance. The ISO 19011 is an international standard that sets forth guidelines for management systems auditing[3]. This book presents many auditing tools and techniques needed when conducting effective internal and external audits. An audit can be conducted against a range of audit criteria, separately or in combination, including:

- Requirements defined in one or more management system standards.
- Policies and requirements specified by relevant interested parties.
- Statutory and regulatory requirements.

---

[1] 21 CFR § 820.22
[2] ICH Q10: Pharmaceutical Quality System, § 4.1
[3] ISO 19011 (2018): Guidelines for Auditing Management Systems

- One or more management system processes defined by the organization or other parties.
- Management system plan(s) relating to the provision of specific outputs of a management system.

This book provides guidance for all sizes and types of organizations and audits of varying scopes and scales, including those conducted by large audit teams, typically of larger organizations, and those by single auditors, whether in large or small organizations. The material presented here should be adapted as appropriate to the scope, complexity, and scale of the audit program. The book concentrates on internal audits conducted by personnel of the audited organization (first party) and audits conducted by organizations on their external providers and other external interested parties (second party). This document can also be useful for external audits conducted for purposes other than third-party management system certification.

The material presented through this book is intended to apply to a broad range of potential users, including auditors, organizations implementing management systems and organizations needing to conduct management system audits for contractual or regulatory reasons. Users can, however, apply the material presented when developing their own audit-related requirements. It can also be used for the purpose of self-declaration and can be useful to organizations involved in auditor training or personnel certification.

The book is organized in eight chapters and various appendices, which provide extra materials to be used by any person during the audit process. Chapter 1 provides some audit basics, such as the audit stages, the general types of audits, and the classification of audits based on where they are performed and who performs the audits. Chapter 2 is focused on auditor qualifications. Most of this chapter is based on the guidances provided by the ISO 19011 standard. Then, Chapter 3 presents the expected roles and responsibilities for the different key players involved in the audit process. In Chapter 4, the main elements of the audit checklist are presented, with a detailed description for each of these elements.

Chapters 5 to 8 focus on the four stages of the audit process. Specifically, Chapter 5 presents the main elements of the audit planning stage, including the main elements of the audit plan. Then, Chapter 6 presents the details of the audit performance stage, beginning with the opening meeting and finishing with the closing meeting. Chapter 7 presents the most common elements of an audit report, along with some important hints about what to include and what to exclude from the audit report. Chapter 8 is about the follow-up stage of the audit process. Due to the increased frequency of virtual audits, Chapter 9 presents important considerations for these types of audits. Finally, Chapter 10 presents the elements of internal audits certification, as provided by Business Excellence Consulting Inc. as part of our training curricula.

The book also includes five appendices. Appendix A shows a template for a procedure of auditor qualification. Appendix B presents a template of an auditor's record of qualification. Then, Appendix C shows the criteria used for the scoring system of the auditor's record of qualification. An example of an audit report template is presented in Appendix D. Finally, the practice exercises provided during Business Excellence Consulting Inc.'s internal audits certification is presented in Appendix E.

More information about our consulting, training, and auditing services can be accessed at www.bec-global.com.

Acronyms and Definitions

Audit: systematic, independent, and documented process for obtaining objective evidence and evaluating it objectively to determine the extent to which the audit criteria are fulfilled.

Audit client: organization or person requesting an audit.

Audit conclusion: outcome of an audit, after consideration of the audit objectives and all audit findings.

Audit criteria: set of requirements used as a reference against which objective evidence is compared.

Audit evidence: records, statements of fact or other information, which are relevant to the audit criteria and verifiable.

Audit findings: results of the evaluation of the collected audit evidence against audit criteria.

Audit plan: description of the activities and arrangements for an audit.

Audit program: arrangements for a set of one or more audits planned for a specific time frame and directed towards a specific purpose.

Audit scope: extent and boundaries of an audit.

Audit team: one or more persons conducting an audit, supported if needed by technical experts.

Auditing organization: a group or individual who performs audits as a business.

Auditee: organization as a whole or parts thereof being audited.

Auditor: person who conducts an audit.

Competence: ability to apply knowledge and skills to achieve intended results.

Compliance: an affirmative indication or judgement that the auditee has met the specified requirements.

Conformance: indication that a product or service has met the requirements.

Defect: departure of a quality characteristic from the specifications.

Defective: unit of product containing at least one defect.

Effectiveness: extent to which planned activities are realized and planned results achieved.

Finding: a conclusion of importance based on observations.

Management system: set of interrelated or interacting elements of an organization to establish policies and objectives, and processes to achieve those objectives.

Nonconformity: non-fulfilment of a requirement.

Objective evidence: data supporting the existence or verity of something. Information or statement of fact based on observation or measurement which can be verified.

Observation: a statement of fact made during an audit and substantiated by objective evidence.

Observer: individual who accompanies the audit team but does not act as an auditor.

Performance: measurable result.

Process: set of interrelated or interacting activities that use inputs to deliver an intended result.

Requirement: need or expectation that is stated, generally implied or obligatory.

Technical expert: person who provides specific knowledge or expertise to the audit team.

Chapter 1:
Audit Basics

A n audit is a systematic, independent, and documented process for obtaining objective evidence and evaluating it objectively to determine the extent to which the audit criteria are fulfilled. Auditing is also a powerful management tool in determining how effectively a company controls the quality of its products or services and ensures compliance with the established requirements.

There are many individuals who participate through all the stages of the audit process. However, the key players in an audit are the audit client, the auditor(s), and the auditee. The *audit client* is the person or organization that has the authority to initiate the audit. It is the individual or job function who starts the auditing process. The *auditors* are the individuals who carry out the audit, following the audit principles and techniques. Finally, the *auditee* is the person or organization being audited. The roles and responsibilities of each of these key players are presented in Chapter 3.

1.1 Audit Stages

Audits must be well planned, documented, formal, and systematic. To visualize the audit process in a systematic way, we can divide it into the following four stages:

- Planning or Preparation

- Performance or Execution
- Reporting
- Follow-Up

This book will present the details for each of these four stages in Chapters 5 to 8. For now, a brief description of the most relevant details of each stage are presented here:

Planning or Preparation

In this stage, the initial conversations between the audit client and the auditing organization begin. An audit team leader is appointed by the auditing organization for the specific audit. It is the audit client who defines the audit objective, scope, tentative dates, and communicate them to the audit team leader. Then, the audit team leader initiates the communication with the auditee's management representative to provide those agreements reached with the audit client. The details of this stage are presented in Chapter 5.

Performance or Execution

This is the stage in which the audit activities at the auditee are carried out. It begins with an opening meeting and ends with the closing meeting. During the audit process, data collection activities such as interviews and field work are conducted. Besides the opening and closing meetings, other types of meetings also occur during this stage: daily briefings between the audit team and the auditee's management, and caucus meetings among the audit team members. The details of this stage are presented in Chapter 6.

Reporting

During the closing meeting, a draft audit report is presented to the auditee's top management representatives. It is important to realize that the draft report it is not the final audit report, which will be submitted to the client a few weeks after the closing meeting. The main purpose of leaving a draft report to the auditee at the closing meeting is to provide a starting point for the auditee to start working on the improvement opportunities identified thorough the audit process. The details of this stage are presented in Chapter 7.

Follow-Up

The final stage of the audit process is the follow-up. The main purpose of the follow-up stage is to verify if the actions required by the auditee to address the audit findings were implemented, and if those actions were effective. This is sometimes considered the weakest link of the audit process. The follow-up stage will depend on many factors, including the type of audit, who performs the audit, and the audit location, among others. The details of this stage are presented in Chapter 8.

1.2 General Types of Audits

Sometimes, we hear about many types of audits. For example, management audits, vendor audits, compliance audits, surveillance audits, certification audits, and so on. However, in general, audits can be categorized in any of the following three categories: system audit, process audit, or product audit. The audit scope is what determines the type of audit. As previously mentioned, it is the audit client who determines the audit scope. Let us describe each of the three types of audits.

System Audit

This is the most comprehensive type of audit. A system audit covers all the elements of the system being audited: quality system, safety system, environmental system, financial system, and so on. Because the system audit is the most comprehensive type of audit, it will require more auditors, longer duration, and more planning than the other types of audits. A system audit can take a few days or weeks to be completed and will often require more than two or three auditors. For example, the registration audit for the ISO 9001 standard is considered a system audit. Also, our accreditation audit for the ANSI-IACET 1-2018 standard is a system audit. Usually, many organizations perform process audits on a weekly or monthly basis but perform a full system audit on a yearly basis. Some system audits can be performed on a less frequent basis. For example, every two or three years. The frequency of the system audits must be established by the audit client.

Process Audit

This is the most common type of audit. A process audit can focus on one or more processes at the same time. For example, a process audit can be conducted in any area of the organization: receiving warehouse, manufacturing, packaging, laboratory, purchasing, accounting, and so on. The process audit is less extensive than system audits, but more extensive than product audits. For this reason, the required resources will be less for this type of audit than for the system audit, but more than for the product audit. A process audit can take a few hours or days to be completed and can often be conducted by one or two auditors.

Product Audit

This is the least extensive type of audit; thus, it requires less resources than both the system and process audits. This type of audit is performed on the final product; however, it is important to say the product audit is not a substitute for the final inspection. Usually, the product audit is performed at the finished goods warehouse to determine if the product complies with all requirements: quality, packaging, labeling, quantity, and so on. Sometimes, the product audit is referred as "customer-oriented" audit. A product audit can take a few hours to be completed and can often be conducted by one auditor.

1.3 Where Are the Audits Performed

Many times, we hear the words "internal audit" and "external audit".

This situation creates confusion because we think that internal audits are only those audits performed by the auditee organization using their own auditors. That type of audit is called "first-party internal audit". However, as we will see in Section 1.4, "where" the audit is performed should not be confused with "who" performs the audit. For simplicity, let us categorize the place where the audits are performed as internal audits and external audits.

Internal Audits

As mentioned earlier, many times the audits performed by the auditee using their own auditors are referred to internal audits. However, that is partially true. Why? If we bring someone from corporate to audit our processes, or if we hire an independent auditor to audit our processes, those are also considered internal audits. However, the difference is "who" is performing the audit. In Section 1.4, we will discuss more about the "who" performs the audit.

External Audits

We usually call "external audits" those audits we perform at our supplier's facilities. Also, when we hire an external auditing organization to audit our suppliers, it is also referred to external audit. Both situations are correct. However, how will our suppliers call an audit we perform at their facilities? Internal or external? From their standpoint, it will be an internal audit, but from our standpoint it is an external audit. So, who is correct? Both. Because the main difference between internal and external depends on from whose standpoint it is viewed: the auditor or the auditee.

1.4 Who Performs the Audits

As can be observed in the previous sections, it is a combination of factors and from whose standpoint the audit is seen that will determine if an audit is to be considered an internal audit or an external audit.

Now, let us evaluate "who" performs the audit, from the auditee's standpoint to determine another classification of audits: first-party, second-party, or third-party.

First-Party Audits

When an audit is performed at the auditee's facility using the auditee's resources as auditors (while maintaining the independence principle, which will be discussed later in this book), it is called a first-party audit. In other words, a first-party audit is considered an audit "for the auditee, by the auditee". First-party audits are always internal audits because they are performed at the auditee's facilities.

Second-Party Audits

Every time an organization receives an audit from a customer, or when the organization performs an audit at a supplier's facilities, it is considered a second-party audit. The main difference in both audits is whether it is considered internal or external. For example, when the organization receive an audit from a customer, from the organization's (auditee) standpoint it will be a second-party internal audit. From the customer's (auditor) standpoint, it will be a second-party external audit. However, on the same token, when an organization audit its suppliers, it will be a second-party external audit, from the organization's (auditor) standpoint. But from the supplier's (auditee) standpoint, it will be a second-party internal audit. What if an organization is audited by the corporate office personnel or sister facilities of the same organization? These audits are also considered second-party audits.

Third-Party Audits

There are situations in which an organization wants to be audited by an independent organization, which does not have any business relationship with it (customers, suppliers, sister facilities, corporate, and so on). This type of audit is classified as third-party audit. Same as with the second-party audit, the third-party audits can be either internal or external, depending on whose standpoint we are considering. The main difference between second-party and third-party audits is the business relationship between the auditor and the auditee. Third-party audits are useful when an organization wants an independent assessment of their systems, to pursue an accreditation, registration, or certification. An example could be an ISO 9001 registration or an ANSI/IACET 1-2018 accreditation.

Figure 1.1 shows the relationships among the different audits, based on the "where" the audit is conducted and "who" conducts the audit. The "where" is considered from the manufacturer standpoint, using the supplier-manufacturer-customer relationship. For example, the first-party internal audit is performed by the manufacturer within the manufacturer's facilities. When the customer audits the manufacturer, it will be a second-party internal audit (from the manufacturer's standpoint); however, when the manufacturer audits the supplier, it will also be a second-party audit, but external (from the manufacturer's standpoint). Similar situations happen when it is an independent auditing organization which audits the manufacturer (third-party internal) or when the manufacturer hires an independent auditing organization to audit suppliers on their behalf (third-party external). The classifications of audits presented in this section apply regardless of the scope of the audit: system, process, or product audit. As can be seen, sometimes classifying an audit can be unclear. It depends on the scope, where is the audit performed, and who performs the audit.

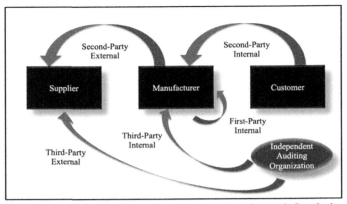

Figure 1.1: Classification of Audits from the Manufacturer's Standpoint

1.5 Audit Purpose and Objectives

The purpose of quality auditing is to examine the effectiveness of management-directed control programs. Therefore, the philosophy of quality assurance programs is based on prevention rather than detection of problems. In other words, the purpose of quality auditing is to identify and address improvement opportunities before they become a nonconformance or noncompliance.

The audit purpose and objective are defined by the audit client and communicated to the lead auditor during the planning stage of the audit. Later during the same stage, the lead auditor communicates the purpose and objective to the auditee's management representative. A quality management system audit should meet one or more of the following objectives:

- Determine the conformity or nonconformity of the quality system clauses.
- Determine the effectiveness of the implemented quality system in meeting specified quality objectives.
- Provide the auditee with the opportunity to improve the quality system.

8

- Meet regulatory requirements
- Permit the listing of the audited organization's quality system in a register.

1.6 Audit Evidence

During the performance or execution stage, the auditors collect evidence through various mechanisms, such as interviews and field work. Evidence is any information that can be proved true, based on facts obtained through observation, measurement, test, or other means. The three types of evidence that auditors collect during the audit can be classified as:

- **Testimonial evidence:** information obtained by interviewing the parties involved within the process, such as the operators, supervisors, mechanics, technicians, and so on.
- **Documentary evidence:** information obtained by reviewing documents, such as production batch records, forms, drawings, device master records, and so on.
- **Subject-matter expert evidence:** information obtained by interviewing persons who are not directly involved in the process but, because of their expertise, they can formulate hypothesis and reach conclusions based on scientific evaluation of the data.

Although the auditors will make their best efforts to obtain evidence during the audit, the absence of evidence on the auditee's part is not necessary evidence on the auditor's part. In other words, the adage "silence is consent" does not apply to the audit process. Also, it is perfectly acceptable to allow verbal evidence when evidence on the contrary cannot be substantiated. However, most management systems specifically require some documented (written) evidence as part of the records needed to support compliance with the quality system requirements.

At this point, it is important to explain the difference between an observation and a finding, which are part of the evidence which will be obtained during the audit. An *observation* is a statement of fact made during an audit and substantiated by objective evidence. Then, a *finding* is a conclusion of importance based on observations. Findings can be conformities or nonconformities, and can be expressed either quantitatively or qualitatively, or both. For example, an observation could be something like "two documents were found with missing signatures in Department A". Another observation could be "three documents were found with missing signatures in Department B". A third observation could be "One document was found with missing signatures in Department C". Each one of these, individually, is an observation. However, the finding (or conclusion) could be expressed in this way: "The approval and review process is inadequate". In this way, the actions to address the finding must cover the observations identified in those three departments (corrective actions), but also an effort must be made to avoid the occurrence of the failure in other departments (preventive actions).

1.7 Analysis of Audit Nonconformities

Once the findings have been identified, they must be grouped into pre-defined categories. Some of the categories in which findings can be grouped are:

- Documentation issues
- Process control issues
- Calibration issues
- Training issues
- Material control issues
- Inspection issues

As will be explained in a later chapter, during the post-audit preparation meeting, the auditors classify the grouped findings, based on their risk. A typical classification of audit findings is:

- **Critical:** failure may have an impact on the health or safety of any person.
- **Major:** failure might affect the general function of the product, not causing any harm to the person.
- **Minor:** failure does not affect the function of the product. They are cosmetic or incidental.

Table 1.1 shows an example of the three findings classifications, along with some definitions for each classification, and recommended actions for each finding classification.

Table 1.1: Classification of Findings

Classification	Definition	Recommended Action from Auditee
Critical	A deficiency which has produced or leads to a significant risk of producing either a product which is harmful to the patient or the business. Condition or issue that could directly affect the identity, strength, quality, and purity of the product, could pose an immediate or latent health risk, could lead to action by regulatory authorities, including withholding	Immediate corrective action is mandatory. A time schedule for CAPA implementation is required.

Critical (cont.)	approval of a pending application. Also, any observation that involves fraud, misrepresentation or falsification of product or data. Several related major deficiencies may be taken together to constitute a critical deficiency and will be reported as such.	
Major	A non-critical deficiency that has produced or may result in a product that does not comply with marketing authorization or the Quality Agreement; indicates a major deviation from the Code of cGMP; indicates a failure to carry out satisfactory procedures or release of batches; or a systematic pattern of non- compliance which collectively constitutes a major observation. Several related minor deficiencies may be taken together to constitute a major deficiency and will be reported as such.	A time schedule for CAPA implementation is required.

Minor	A deficiency but which indicates a departure from cGMP where no potential impact (direct or indirect) to the product is evident.; a deficiency for which there is insufficient information to classify it as major or critical.	A time schedule for CAPA implementation is recommended.

Chapter 2:
Auditor Qualifications

The ISO 19011:2018 standard establishes that confidence in the audit process and the ability to achieve its objectives depends on the competence of those individuals who are involved in performing audits, including auditors and audit team leaders. Competence should be evaluated regularly through a process that considers personal attributes and the ability to apply the knowledge and skills gained through education, work experience, auditor training and audit experience. This process must consider the needs of the audit program and its objectives. Some of the knowledge and skills described in Chapter 2.3 are common to auditors of any management system discipline; others are specific to individual management system disciplines. It is not necessary for each auditor in the audit team to have the same competence. However, the overall competence of the audit team needs to be sufficient to achieve the audit objectives. The evaluation of auditor competence should be planned, implemented, and documented to provide an outcome that is objective, consistent, fair, and reliable.

2.1 Qualification Criteria for Auditors

Auditor competence can be acquired using a combination of the following factors:

15

- Successfully completing training programs that cover generic auditor knowledge and skills. Successful completion of a training course will depend on the type of course. For courses with an examination component, it can mean successfully passing the examination. For other courses, it can mean participating in and completing the course.
- Experience in a relevant technical, managerial, or professional position involving the exercise of judgement, decision making, problem solving and communication with managers, professionals, peers, customers, and other relevant interested parties.
- Education/training and experience in a specific management system discipline and sector that contribute to the development of overall competence.
- Audit experience acquired under the supervision of an auditor competent in the same discipline.

Table 2.1 shows an example of the expected parameters to be considered during the qualification of auditors and some recommendations for each parameter.

Table 2.1: Auditor Qualification Criteria

Parameter	Recommendation
Education	Secondary school education
Total work experience	5 years
Work experience in quality management	At least 2 years of the total 5 years
Auditor training	Lead auditor training
Audit experience	4 complete audits for a total of 20 days of audit experience as an auditor-in-training, with the direction and guidance of an audit team leader

Appendix A presents a template for a procedure for auditor qualification. Then, Appendix B shows a template of a *Record for Auditor Qualification*, and Appendix C shows an example of the *Scoring System for the Record of Auditor Qualification*.

2.2 Personal Attributes

Auditors should possess the necessary attributes to enable them to act in accordance with the principles of auditing. Auditors should exhibit professional behavior during the performance of audit activities. Desired professional behaviors include being[4]:

- **Ethical:** fair, truthful, sincere, honest, and discreet.
- **Open-minded:** willing to consider alternative ideas or points of view.
- **Diplomatic:** tactful in dealing with individuals.
- **Observant:** actively observing physical surroundings and activities.
- **Perceptive:** aware of and able to understand situations.
- **Versatile:** able to readily adapt to different situations.
- **Tenacious:** persistent and focused on achieving objectives.
- **Decisive:** able to reach timely conclusions based on logical reasoning and analysis.
- **Self-reliant:** able to act and function independently while interacting effectively with others.
- **Able to act with fortitude:** able to act responsibly and ethically, even though these actions may not always be popular and may sometimes result in disagreement or confrontation.
- **Open to improvement:** willing to learn from situations.

---

[4] ISO 19011:2018, § 7.2.2.

- **Culturally sensitive:** observant and respectful to the culture of the auditee.
- **Collaborative:** effectively interacting with others, including audit team members and the auditee's personnel.

2.3 Knowledge and Skills of Auditors

Auditors should possess the knowledge and skills necessary to achieve the intended results of the audits they are expected to perform. They also need the generic competence and a level of discipline and sector-specific knowledge and skills. Auditors should have knowledge and skills in the areas outlined below:

- Audit principles, processes, and methods: knowledge and skills in this area enable the auditor to ensure audits are performed in a consistent and systematic manner.
- Management system standards and other references: knowledge and skills in this area enable the auditor to understand the audit scope and apply audit criteria.
- The organization and its context: knowledge and skills in this area enable the auditor to understand the auditee's structure, purpose, and management practices.
- Applicable statutory and regulatory requirements and other requirements: knowledge and skills in this area enable the auditor to be aware of, and work within, the organization's requirements.

2.4 Knowledge and Skills of Audit Team Leader

To facilitate the efficient and effective conduct of the audit, an audit team leader should have the competence to:

- Plan the audit and assign audit tasks according to the specific competence of individual audit team members.
- Discuss strategic issues with top management of the auditee to determine whether they have considered these issues when evaluating their risks and opportunities.
- Develop and maintain a collaborative working relationship among the audit team members.
- Manage the audit process, including:
  o Making effective use of resources during the audit.
  o Managing the uncertainty of achieving audit objectives.
  o Protecting the health and safety of the audit team members during the audit, including ensuring compliance of the auditors with the relevant health and safety, and security arrangements.
  o Directing the audit team members.
  o Providing direction and guidance to auditors-in-training.
  o Preventing and resolving conflicts and problems that can occur during the audit, including those within the audit team, as necessary.
- Represent the audit team in communications with the individual(s) managing the audit program, the audit client, and the auditee.
- Lead the audit team to reach the audit conclusions.
- Prepare and complete the audit report.

2.5 Maintenance and Improvement of Competence

Auditors and audit team leaders should continually improve their competence. Auditors should maintain their auditing competence through regular participation in management system audits and continual professional development. This may be achieved through means such as additional work experience, training, private study, coaching, attendance at meetings, seminars and conferences or other relevant activities. The individual(s) managing the audit program should establish suitable mechanisms for the continual evaluation of the performance of the auditors and audit team leaders. The continual professional development activities must consider the following:

- Changes in the needs of the individual and the organization responsible for the conduct of the audit.
- Developments in the practice of auditing including the use of technology.
- Relevant standards including guidance/supporting documents and other requirements
- Changes in sector or disciplines.

2.6 Auditor Evaluation

Evaluation of auditors and audit team leaders must be planned, implemented, and recorded. That evaluation must occur during the following stages: initial evaluation, audit team selection process, and continual evaluation of auditor performance. The criteria should be qualitative (such as having demonstrated desired behavior, knowledge, or the performance of the skills, in training or in the workplace) and quantitative (such as the years of work experience and education, number of audits conducted, hours of audit training). Table 2.2 shows some examples of evaluation methods for auditors[5].

---

[5] ISO 19011:2018, § 7.4.

Table 2.2: Auditor Evaluation Methods

Evaluation method	Objectives	Examples
Review of records	To verify the background of the auditor.	Analysis of records of education, training, professional credentials, and auditing experience.
Feedback	To provide information about how the performance of the auditor is perceived.	Surveys, questionnaires, personal references, testimonials, complaints, performance evaluation, peer review.
Interview	To evaluate desired professional behavior and communication skills, to verify information and test knowledge.	Personal interviews.
Observation	To evaluate desired professional behavior and the ability to apply knowledge and skills.	Role playing, witnessed audits, on-the-job performance.
Testing	To evaluate desired behavior and knowledge and skills and their application.	Oral and written exams, psychometric testing.
Post-audit review	To provide information on the auditor performance during the audit activities, identify strengths and opportunities for improvement.	Review of the audit report, interviews with the audit team leader, the audit team and, if appropriate, feedback from the auditee.

Chapter 3:
Roles and Responsibilities
of Auditors

As presented in Chapter 1, during the audit there are various key players involved. They can be classified into three major classifications: audit client, auditors, and auditee. Each of these key players have specific roles and responsibilities during the various stages of the audit process.

3.1 Audit Roles and Responsibilities

To guarantee a smooth flow of activities throughout the audit process, roles and responsibilities of each participant must be clearly defined. Some of the main responsibilities for each of the key players during the audit process are, but not limited to:

- **Audit Client:** is responsible to determine the audit need, scope, and objective; then, communicate them to the lead auditor. It is the person who receives the audit report, unless otherwise specified. The audit client is who determines the type of follow-up for each of the findings included in the audit report.
- **Auditor:** is responsible to comply with the applicable audit requirements and documenting and reporting the audit results. The auditor must maintain the confidential nature of the audit.

- **Auditee:** is responsible to provide the resources needed during the audit and provide access to the facilities and materials, as requested by the auditors. The auditee is who determines and initiate the corrective actions to address the audit findings.

Another key player, specifically during the audit performance or execution stage is the *escort*. This person acts as a liaison between the auditors and the auditee. Some of the main responsibilities of the escort are:

- Provide cooperation and assistance.
- Provide a central location for the audit.
- Review the auditor's observations and findings.
- Inform auditors about any proprietary or confidential material.
- Plan for auditee interview and arrange requested meetings.
- Convey areas of concerns to the auditee management.

Many organizations do not pay too much attention to this important resource. The probability of success or failure of an audit lies, in part, in the interaction between the escorts with auditors, and eventually their interaction with the auditee's management. For example, because the escorts will probably be the first auditee representatives who become knowledgeable about specific audit findings, they can communicate those findings immediately to the auditee management and start addressing those findings before the end of the audit. In some instances, a minor finding which has been already fixed before then end of the audit performance stage is not included as part of the audit report. However, this is discretionary on the part of the lead auditor.

3.2 Auditor Independence and Objectivity

One of the most important aspects to address during all the stages of the audit process is auditor independence, which helps to maintain the integrity of the audit and the validity of the audit report. The audit organization must be free of restrictive influences from their own company management or from auditee management in the performance or reporting of the audit. Auditors must not have preconceived opinions or hold bias toward the function, department, or system being audited. Although the organizational hierarchy can play an important role to establish auditor independence, the true independence of the audit function is reflected in the quality and objectivity of the audit report.

Audits must always be based on objective and verifiable facts. For this reason, being an objective auditor pertains to gathering the facts as they are presented or uncovered during the audit. Therefore, imposing any corrective action where one is not needed can be highly detrimental to all parties concerned.

3.3 Audit Conflict Resolution

Many times, during the performance or execution stage of the audit, the auditors are faced with conflicting situations. The way in which conflict is managed play an important role in the success of the audit. Some of the most common conflict situations an auditor might find during the audit are antagonism, defensive behavior, auditee time wasters, and lack of auditee commitment. A brief explanation of each, and ways to manage them is presented here:

- **Antagonism** happens many times when the auditor's authority is not recognized by the auditee. In this type of situation, the best approach is to involve the audit client since the early stages of the audit process to make the auditee aware of the importance of the audit and delegate the authority to identify the opportunity areas to the auditors. In this way, auditee will recognize the auditor's authority at all stages of the audit process.

- **Defensive behavior** happens mostly because the auditee either does not know the answer to an auditor's question or does not want to answer the question. A defensive "threat" response from the auditee may be an indicator that a noncompliance exists. In a situation like this, it is very important to let the auditee know that the biggest benefit of the audit result is for the auditee, not for the auditors. So, by providing the information requested by the auditors, opportunity areas can be identified and addressed for the benefit of the auditee.

- **Auditee time waster** is a very common situation, which jeopardizes the audit agenda; thus, having a negative impact on the established time to complete the audit and provide the results to the audit client and auditee's management. Some of the most frequent time wasters are the delay to submit documentation requested by the auditors and the long lunch. To avoid this, auditors usually have their lunch and breaks in the working area provided to them. Also, auditors must notify the auditee that any delay in the submission of information requested by the auditors could delay the completion of the audit as per the agreed schedule.

- **Lack of auditee commitment** usually is reflected in the delay of submitting information requested by auditors and not providing all the resources required for an effective completion of the audit. In this situation, the best approach is to let the auditee know that lack of commitment could result in a negative impact to the audit's results. If auditee does not respond adequately, then the issue must be escalated to the audit client for resolution.

Chapter 4:
The Audit Checklist

The checklist is one of the most important working documents of the auditor. The use of checklists during the audit has many benefits, such as keeping the audit on schedule and flowing smoothly, using the audit time efficiently, and allow thorough coverage of the audit scope, among others. Checklists can be categorized as scoring on non-scoring.

Scoring checklists are based on assigning scores to each element evaluated during the audit. An example of the use of this type of checklist is the Malcolm Baldrige National Quality Award. The audit criteria for this award are divided in seven elements and each element has a maximum achievable score. Then, each element is evaluated, and a score given to every element based on how compliance to the requirements is met. Finally, a minimum score is established to pass the assessment. The same approach for scoring checklists has been defined by many organizations to be used during the audits. However, the main disadvantages to scoring checklists are:

- Developing the score and achieving consistency when applying the criteria to assign a score is very difficult.
- Passing the audit with the minimum required score does not promote continuous improvement.

Non-scoring checklists are the most common type of checklist used during audits. Their main difference to scoring checklists is that they do not assign a numerical value to the response. Their focus is on asking questions about the elements to be audited and collecting the responses to those answers. Compliance or noncompliance to the element's requirements are based without having to assign a specific value to the response. Because of their simplicity, training in the use of non-scoring checklists should be easier than for scoring checklists.

4.1 Purpose of the Audit Checklist

The main purpose of the audit checklist is to guide the auditors during the interviews to collect objective evidence. To achieve this purpose, the checklist must clearly identify the element's requirements being evaluated. Although many organizations develop standard checklists to be used for different audits, the checklists must meet the unique needs of the auditors for each specific audit. For example, the questions in an audit checklist for a specific process might not apply for other processes. Many organizations simply add a "non-applicable" (N/A) choice to cover this situation. However, I have seen situations in which as much as 70% of the questions in a specific checklist were marked with "N/A". So, my recommendation is to tailor the checklists for each audit, and standardize as much as possible, but do not have a generic checklist for all your audits.

4.2 Benefits and Risks of Audit Checklists

As mentioned earlier, the use of checklists during the audit has many benefits, such as keeping the audit on schedule and flowing smoothly, using the audit time efficiently, and allow thorough coverage of the audit scope. All these factors provide confidence in the completeness of the audit. Because checklists are developed during the planning stage of the audit (prior to the performance or execution stage), the use of checklists provides consistency when audits are performed by a variety of individuals and provide a baseline of requirements that remains consistent over time. Using checklist questions results in audits which are thorough, effective, and uniform. Checklists help to assure that the appropriate and necessary questions are asked, and that evidence is examined where needed. It is important to recognize that the checklist is only a guide. It should never be a substitute for good interview techniques, as discussed in Chapter 6.5.

The use of checklists also entails some risks, which must not be overlooked. For example, by just asking the questions included in a checklist, it may discourage the use of additional probing questions, as explained in Chapter 6.5. This could create a "tunnel vision" on both the auditors and auditees, which could limit the interview process only to pre-determined questions. Another risk in the use of checklist is that, after certain number of audits, the auditee can anticipate audit questions. However, this is not detrimental to the audit because if an auditee can anticipate the questions, they could start improving the processes before the audit begins.

4.3 Contents of the Audit Checklist

Audit checklists must contain the requirements to be evaluated to determine if the process complies or not complies with those requirements. As mentioned earlier, ideally, an auditor must ask open-ended questions during the interviews, because they provide for more detailed answers than close-ended questions. Audit checklists that contain only close-ended questions can create a problem to the auditor because the answer would be just a "yes" or "no", without any further details about the answer. For example, when an auditor asks: "*Do you have training records?*", the answer will be either "yes" or "no". If the answer is "no", the auditor can immediately identify a deficiency in the system; however, if the answer is "yes", the auditor will not have an idea if the training records are adequate, if they are updated, if they are kept for all the personnel, and so on. In this case, it is better to combine some close-ended questions with other open-ended questions such as: *"How long do you keep your training records?"*

There is no standardized checklist format for all types of audits. However, as a minimum, a good checklist must contain the following elements:

- **Question number:** a unique number, in ascending order to identify each question.
- **Requirement number:** the identification of the requirement, such as section of the standard or the procedure being evaluated thorough that specific questions. For example, *"Section 4.1.3 of procedure ABC-123, Rev. B."*
- **Requirement:** a brief description of the requirement being evaluated. For example, *"All operators must comply with 8 hours of Current Good Manufacturing Practices each year."* It is important to realize the requirement must be written in such a measurable way that makes it easy for the auditor to determine compliance or noncompliance in an objective way. That is, the requirement must not be subject to interpretation, either from the auditor or the auditee, or both. The requirement could be expressed in sentence format or question format.
- **Evidence:** in this element of the checklist, the auditor includes all the objective evidence related to the compliance or noncompliance to the "Requirement" element. Examples of objective evidence can be obtained from procedures, forms, graphs, charts, examples, observations, statements of facts, and so on.
- **Audit Notes:** in this part of the checklist, the auditor may include any other relevant information which have not been included in the other elements. Some examples are follow-up activities the auditor feels necessary, additional investigation pathways, who else the auditor wants to talk about the findings, and any additional note the auditor considers appropriate.

Table 4.1 shows an example of a checklist template, with all the elements previously discussed, that can be used during the objective evidence collection.

Table 4.1: Audit Checklist Template

#	Requirement no.	Requirement	Evidence	Audit Notes
1				
2				
3				
4				
5				
6				
7				
8				
9				
10				

Chapter 5:
Planning Audits

As discussed in Chapter 1.1, the audit process can be divided into four stages: planning, performance, reporting, and follow-up. In this chapter we will focus on the first stage: audit planning. The audit process formally starts when the audit client contacts the auditing organization to request that an audit be performed to the auditee. The auditing organization will identify an audit team leader, or lead auditor, who will be the person responsible to lead all the stages of the audit process.

5.1 Initiating the Audit

The audit client is the person who defines the audit objective, scope, and expected dates for the audit. The audit client also determines the frequency of the audit, based on the importance of the activity, using a risk-based approach. Once established, any changes to the audit objective, scope, expected dates, or audit frequency must be agreed by the client and the audit team leader.

The audit objective should specify what is to be accomplished. Some examples of audit objectives are to:

- Determine the conformity or nonconformity of the quality system clauses.

- Determine the effectiveness of the implemented quality system in meeting specified quality objectives.
- Provide the auditee with the opportunity to improve the quality system.
- Meet regulatory requirements
- Permit the listing of the audited organization's quality system in a register.

The scope of the audit determines the type of audit: system, process, or product. Based on the audit scope, the audit team leader will determine how many auditors will be required to conduct the audit and will be able to tailor the checklist to cover those areas within the scope of the audit. Some considerations for determining the size and composition of the audit team are:

- Audit objectives, scope, criteria, and estimated duration.
- Competence needed to achieve objectives.
- Statutory, regulatory, contractual, and accreditation or certification requirements.
- Independence of the audit team to avoid conflict of interest.
- Ability of the audit team member to interact effectively.
- Technical experts may be assigned to ensure requirements are met.

The audit team leader must assure that auditors have the required competencies to achieve the audit objectives. Selection of audit team members to ensure the necessary knowledge and skills are present may be satisfied by including technical experts. Those technical experts must operate under the direction of an auditor. Many times, auditors-in-training may be included in the audit team as observers. Once the audit team has been defined, either the client or the auditee can request the replacement on reasonable grounds. Such reasons must be communicated to the audit team leader and to the audit program management.

The outcome of the initial conversations among the audit client, the audit team leader, and the auditee is a formal audit plan. The audit team leader must adopt a risk-based approach to planning the audit based on the information in the audit program and the documented information provided by the audit client and the auditee. Audit planning must consider the risks of the audit activities on the auditee's processes and provide the basis for the agreement among the audit client, audit team and the auditee regarding the conduct of the audit. Planning must facilitate the efficient scheduling and coordination of the audit activities to achieve the objectives effectively. Audit plans must be presented to the auditee. Any issues with the audit plans must be resolved between the audit team leader, the auditee, and the audit client.

5.2 Audit Plan Elements

The audit plan is a formal document developed during the planning stage, which must be updated as the audit progresses. The amount of detail provided in the audit plan must reflect the scope and complexity of the audit, as well as the risk of not achieving the audit objectives. The audit plan should cover the following elements:

- Audit objectives and scope
- Audit criteria and reference documents
- Dates and places of on-site audit activities
- Expected time and duration of activities
- Roles and responsibilities
- Allocation of appropriate resources
- Identification of auditee's representative
- Audit report topics
- Logistics (travel, facilities, etc.)

- Matters related to confidentiality
- Audit follow-up actions

5.3 Audit Notification

Once the audit plan is developed between the audit client and the audit team leader, it will be communicated to the auditee through a formal communication process between the audit team leader and the auditee's management designee. In a quality audit, this person is usually the highest-ranking person within the Quality Department. The audit team leader is responsible for conferring with the auditee to reach agreement on audit dates which are acceptable to both parties. Some flexibility to the schedule is permissible. Changes to schedule should be reapproved and redistributed to those impacted by the schedule changes.

The audit team leader must notify the auditee's management designee, in writing, within to three months prior to the conduct of the audit. Advance notification does not hurt the audit; it gives the auditee the opportunity to start improving their control systems before the audit process begins. The formal audit notification must include the following elements:

- Purpose and scope of the audit
- Type of audit
- Dates and duration of the audit
- Auditor names
- Approved checklist questions
- Audit agenda

The audit agenda must show the opening meeting timeframe, the timeframes for the specific audit activities, the names of the auditors assigned to each activity, and the projected time for the closing meeting.

5.4 Conducting Document Review

During the planning stage, the audit team leader will request documents from the auditee to start developing the audit checklists. Some of the documents to be requested from the auditee are procedures, work instructions, drawings, facility's layout, organizational chart, and so on. The document review must consider the size, nature, and complexity of the organization. The audit objectives and scope are also considered as part of the document review. Previous audit reports are sometimes reviewed during this stage.

In some situations, the document review may be deferred until the on-site activities commence, if this is not detrimental to the effectiveness of the conduct of the audit. The audit team leader informs the audit client, audit program management, and the auditee about any inadequate documentation received. When documentation received is inadequate, a decision must be made to continue or suspend the audit until concerns are resolved.

5.5 Preparing for On-Site Activities

During the planning stage, the audit team leader, in consultation with the audit team, assigns responsibility to each team member for auditing processes, functions, sites, areas, or activities. Those assignments take into consideration auditor independence, competence, effective use of resources, and use of technical experts, as required. Although these responsibilities are assigned prior to the beginning of the audit performance stage, changes to work assignments may be made as the audit progresses.

The audit team members are responsible to prepare work documents, as necessary. Those work documents might include checklists, audit sampling plans, and forms for recording information, evidence, findings, and so on. Audit team members are responsible to keep records of meetings held during the audit process. The work documents should be retained at least until the audit completion. Any document involving confidential or proprietary information must be suitable safeguarded by the audit team members.

Chapter 6:
Conducting Audits

A s previously discussed, the audit process can be divided into four stages: planning, performance, reporting, and follow-up. In the previous chapter, the planning stage was discussed. In this chapter, we will discuss the details of the performance stage. The main elements of this stage are:

- Opening meeting
- Audit activities
  - o Interviews
  - o Field work
- Communication during audit
  - o Daily briefings
  - o Caucus meetings
- Closing meeting

6.1 The Opening Meeting

The audit performance stage formally starts with the opening meeting. It is a meeting held between the auditors and the auditee's management, or those persons responsible for the functions or processes to be audited. The purpose of the opening meeting is to provide a short summary of how audit activities will be undertaken. During the opening meeting, the audit plan is confirmed by those in attendance. This meeting, which is also referred as pre-audit meeting, serves to confirm the communication channels that will be followed throughout the audit and to provide the auditee an opportunity to ask questions prior to the beginning of the audit.

The audit team leader is the person who presides the opening meeting. Along with the audit team members, normally all managers or representatives of the areas to be audited should attend. Although the audit client and the auditee's highest-ranking officer may not necessarily attend the opening meeting, they should be invited. The opening meeting for internal audits in small organizations may consist of communicating that an audit is being conducted and explaining the nature of the audit. For other situations, the meeting should be formal, and records of attendance should be kept.

During the opening meeting, the audit team leader will introduce each audit team member, including an outline of their roles within the audit. The auditee's representatives and the audit escorts will also be introduced during the opening meeting. Although the audit objective and scope have been previously discussed during the initial conversations between the audit team leader and the auditee's management designee, they are now presented to the other auditee's representative in charge of the areas being audited. The audit agenda is presented next, along with any last-minute changes to the agenda.

It is also important, at this stage of the process, to explain the methods that will be used during the audit to collect evidence, making clear to the auditee that the conclusions will be based on samples collected during the audit. Not identifying any deficiency does not necessarily mean there are no deficiencies to be identified and corrected by the auditee. Communication channels must also be established during the opening meeting, making the auditee aware that all communication between the auditee and the audit team will be channeled through the audit team leader. Although the audit is usually conducted in the language of the auditee, it is important to establish the language to be used during the audit just in case any translator is required during the process. Ideally, those translators should be provided by the audit team.

Auditee's management must be kept informed at all times during the audit. This will be accomplished through daily briefings between the audit team and the auditee's management. In these daily briefings, the audit team will notify the auditee's management about the progress of the audit, as well as any finding identified up to that point. The auditee's management could also provide the audit team those actions taken to address the identified findings.

The opening meeting is also a good moment to notify the audit team members all relevant work safety, emergency, and security procedures. A private room must be provided to the audit team, as well as escorts who will guide the audit team members through the facility. Finally, at the opening meeting, any conditions for audit termination must be discussed and agreed by the audit team and the auditee's management.

6.2 Communication During the Audit

Communication depends upon the scope and complexity of the audit. The audit team should confer periodically to exchange information, assess audit progress, and reassign work as needed. This type of meeting among the audit team members sometimes is called caucus meeting, or audit team meeting. Any piece of evidence collected during the audit that suggest an immediate and significant risk should be reported without delay to the auditee management.

Also, any concern about an issue outside the audit scope must be discussed with the audit client. Any changes to the audit objective or scope must be conferred with and approved by the audit client. Audit evidence that indicates that audit objectives are unattainable must also be communicated immediately to the audit client, as well as reconfirmation or modification of the audit plan, audit objectives, or audit scope, or termination of the audit.

During the audit performance stage, one of the most important roles is the escort. This person will be the liaison between the auditors and the auditee's management. The escort may accompany the audit team throughout the audit performance stage. However, escorts should not interfere with the audits; they are just there to assist the audit team. Some of the main responsibilities of the escorts are:

- Establishing contact and timing for the interviews.
- Arranging visits to specific parts of the site or organization.
- Ensuring that rules concerning site safety and security procedures are known and respected.
- Witnessing the audit on behalf of the auditee.
- Providing clarification or assisting in collecting information

It is strongly advised that escorts are present during the opening meeting, to meet the auditors in advance of the audit performance stage. However, escorts are not required during the closing meeting because, at this point, they have performed all the tasks for which they are responsible.

6.3 Collecting and Verifying Information During the Audit

All information relevant to the audit objectives, scope, and criteria should be collected by appropriate sampling and should be verified by the auditors and auditee prior to being accepted as audit evidence. Only information that is verifiable may be considered as audit evidence. It must be noted that, because the evidence collected is based on samples, there is always an element of uncertainty during the audit. Therefore, those persons acting upon the audit conclusions should be aware of this uncertainty. During the opening meeting, the audit team leader must notify the auditee's management that, because the audit's conclusions will be based on samples, any opportunity area not identified by the auditors must be addressed and corrected by the auditee.

During the performance stage of the audit, the sources of information may vary according to the scope and complexity of the audit. However, the three types of evidence that will be collected during the audit can be classified as:

- Documentary evidence
- Testimonial evidence
- Subject-matter expert evidence

The documentary evidence will be collected through field work. It can include observation of activities and the surrounding work environment and conditions. Also, field work can include revision of documents, such as policies, plans, procedures, work instructions, standards, specifications, drawings, contracts, orders, and so on. Other types of documents that can be collected and evaluated at this stage are records, such as inspection records, minutes of meetings, audit reports, records of monitoring programs, results of measurements, data summaries, performance indicators, and so on.

On the other side, testimonial evidence and subject-matter expert evidence is typically collected through interviews. Testimonial evidence consists of interviewing the persons related to the areas being audited, such as operators, supervisors, group leaders, mechanics, technicians, and so on. Subject-matter expert evidence is collected by interviewing technical experts which are not necessarily part of the areas being audited. However, based on their expertise, these subject-matter experts can develop hypotheses that can be proved with the data collected during the audit. Another common name for the subject-matter expert evidence is scientific evidence because it is based on scientific knowledge of the people being interviewed.

6.4 Interviews

During the performance stage of the audit, evidence is collected through field work and interviews. It is important to note that interviews should be adapted to the situations and persons being interviewed. Although each interview might be different, there are some common elements that each interview must comply with. For example, the auditors must interview persons from the appropriate organizational levels, depending upon the audit scope and objectives. It means that, among the persons interviewed in a specific area, the auditor should interview upper-level management, mid-level management, lower-level management, operators, technicians, mechanics, and so on. Interviews should be conducted during normal working hours and, whenever possible, at the interviewee's normal workplace. However, sometimes it is better to conduct the interviews in a private setting. Auditors must request the auditee's management, during the opening meeting presentation, a private area to conduct interviews.

For many persons, interviews are a stressful experience. That is why it is very important that auditors use effective techniques during the interview process. For example, to put the interviewee at ease and alleviate any anxiety, explain the reason why you are interviewing the person. Let the interviewee know this is a review of the quality management system, not a job performance evaluation. Also, explain you will be taking notes as you conduct the interview. Note-taking during an audit is the practice of collecting information to provide objective evidence obtained through interviews and observations of personnel, activities, and equipment. Audit note-taking must be accurate so that others can take action. Notes must include information so others can go back and reproduce what was witnessed. Also, notes must be written so the auditor can be able to accurately complete the audit report.

The auditor can initiate the interview by asking the persons to describe their work. When doing so, avoid asking questions that bias the answer. Adequate questions are important to gain information about the process, stimulate the conversation, check agreement with processes and procedures, built rapport between the auditor and interviewee, and to verify information, among others.

Because the interview can be a demanding process, to lessen nervousness of the interviewee about what is being recorded in the checklists, the auditor should read aloud what he/she writes in the response area of each question after information, documentation, and verification is presented. During the evidence collection process, the auditor should determine compliance, but also how adequate compliance is. At the end of the interview, summarize the results, ask if they have any question, and thanks the interviewees for their cooperation.

6.5 Tips for Gathering Information During the Audit

An adequate interview is very important to collect relevant evidence. The following are some of the most common techniques used by auditors during the interviews:

- **Open-ended questions**: these types of questions are those that cannot be answered with just "yes" or "no". Open-ended questions provide more detailed answers than closed-ended questions. For example, asking "*Do you have a procedure to perform this task?*" will lead the interviewee to answer with either "yes" or "no". However, asking "*Which procedure is used to perform this task?*" will let the interviewee provide a more detailed answer, which can be easily followed by another open-ended question. Ideally, most questions during the interview must be open-ended; however, if a close-ended question is asked, then an open-ended question can be asked immediately to get a more elaborated response.
- **Probing**: this type of question is asked to challenge a previous answer. However, the question might be asked in a different

format to determine if the answers provided in both questions are consistent. For example, a question could be *"What are the timeframes to keep training records?"*. Later, the question can be changed to *"Are there different timeframes to keep training records?"*. In this way, consistency of the answers can be evaluated, although the second question was asked using a closed-ended format.

- **Silence**: this is an interesting interviewing technique. It consists of asking a question and, when the interviewee provides the answer, keep silent and looking at the interviewee without asking any other question. This process creates a psychological effect on the interviewee which, thinking that the auditor was expecting a more detailed answer, will start providing more details than originally provided. However, this technique must be sporadically; the auditor must not overuse it.

- **Paraphrasing**: one of the best techniques used to alleviate anxiety of the person being interviewed. When the interviewee provides the answer to a question, the auditor will paraphrase the answer before recording it in the checklist. In this way, the interviewee will make certain the auditor understood the response. Otherwise, if the auditor misunderstood the answer, the interviewee would have a chance to correct the auditor.

All the previous techniques can be used for individual or group interviews. The choice between individual or group interviews depends on many factors. For example, when the auditor wants to contrast the answers of many individuals to specific questions, the individual interview is the best choice. However, when the complete answer cannot be provided by a single individual, a group interview is the preferred choice. An example is when the answer to a question requires knowledge or expertise from different persons, such as operators, technicians, mechanics, and so on. In group interviews, however, it must be stated that supervisors must not interrupt the interview process to provide his/her opinions or answers to a question asked to other persons. Also, when supervisors are present during the interviews, their subordinates might not feel confident to provide honest answers to some questions.

Another consideration for gathering information during the interview process is to explain the interviewee what the auditor is doing and why this is important to the organization. Auditors are fact-finders and they must listen to what the interviewee says. So, the auditor must listen carefully and do not jump to conclusions. The auditors must set aside their own opinions, ideas, and perceptions, and must be open to new information. They should never interrupt the interviewee or walk away before ending the interview. During the interview, the checklists are used as a guidance. Many times, the auditor will need to go beyond the audit checklist, because some answers can lead to other questions not previously included in the checklists.

6.6 Generating Audit Findings

During the performance stage of the audit, different types of evidence (testimonial, documentary, and subject-matter expert) is collected. All audit evidence must be evaluated against the audit criteria, which is the set of requirements used as a reference against which objective evidence is compared. Some examples of audit criteria are policies, procedures, work instructions, standards, regulations, and so on. Conformity or nonconformity to audit criteria must be summarized to indicate locations, functions, or processes that were audited.

Individual audit findings of conformity or nonconformity, and their supporting evidence, must be clearly identified. Those nonconformities may be graded; that is, assigning a quantitative or qualitative classification. It is important to review the nonconformities with the auditee's management to obtain acknowledgment that audit evidence is accurate and understood by the auditors. Also, at this stage, there must be an attempt to resolve any diverging opinions between the auditors and auditee regarding audit evidence and/or findings before the closing meeting. Any unresolved items should be recorded for future discussion between the auditors and auditee.

6.7 Preparing Audit Conclusions

After the data collection process of the performance stage is concluded, the audit team must hold a private meeting to prepare for the presentation of the draft audit report that will be presented during the closing meeting. The audit team should have been working on the development of the draft audit report as the audit progressed. At this moment, the auditors must review the audit findings and other appropriate information collected during the audit. The final audit team meeting is used to reach consensus among auditors on findings, finalize the audit results, and start developing the draft report. This may be done in handwritten or computer format. The draft report should be copied for distribution during the closing meeting.

Audit conclusions can address issues such as the extent of conformity of the management system; effective implementation, maintenance, and improvement of the management systems; capability of the management review to ensure the continuity, adequacy, effectiveness, and improvement. Sometimes, especially during first-party audits, the audit conclusions can lead to recommendations from the auditors regarding improvements, business relationships, certification, registration, or future auditing activities. However, auditor's recommendation should be kept to a minimum because, when the auditors provide recommendations for improvement, their independence could be compromised if they must also have to evaluate the effectiveness of the recommendations they made.

6.8 The Closing Meeting

The last part of the audit performance stage is the closing meeting, also referred as exit meeting or post-audit meeting. The audit team leader, also referred as lead auditor, presides the closing meeting. The main purpose of this meeting is to present the audit findings to the auditee's senior management. Among the auditee's representatives required at this meeting are the staff who have the authority to make the necessary changes to address the corrective action requests. The audit client may or may not attend the closing meeting, because the final audit report must be sent directly to the audit client, unless he/she decides that the audit report is sent directly to the auditee. Attendance records of the closing meeting must be kept and made part of the audit documentation.

During the closing meeting, some concerns might arise and must be discussed between the audit team and the auditee. For example, any clarification of the findings might be requested by the auditee's management at this point. Also, after the corrective action requests are presented by the auditors, the auditee might have some questions regarding those requests, including known difficulties with the submission of timely corrective actions to the auditor's evaluation. During the closing meeting, the establishment of follow-up audits, if applicable, must be discussed and agreed by the audit team and the auditee's management representatives.

Chapter 7:
Audit Report

The formal report is the product of the audit. The audit team leader is responsible for the content and accuracy of the audit report, and for submitting the formal report to the audit client in a timely fashion. Although the report should ideally be signed by all auditors, the only required signature is that of the audit team leader; all the other signatures are optional. The formal audit report is usually submitted to the audit client who, on the other side, is responsible for receiving and distributing the report to the auditee's management. Usually, along with the audit report, the audit team leader includes an acknowledgement form that must be signed by the audit client and sent back to the audit team leader as evidence that the final report was received by the audit client.

7.1 Main Elements of the Audit Report

Although there is not any unique audit report format, the following information is suggested content for the report:

- Cover sheet
  - o Title and date
  - o Executive Summary
- Main body of the report
- Findings and objective evidence
- Requests for corrective actions (where applicable)

The main body section of the report must start with one or two introductory paragraphs, which include the name of the auditee organization, audited facility location, audit purpose and scope, audit dates, and audit team members. It is also suggested to start with a statement about the tone of the audit. In this statement, the auditors must start providing thanks to the auditee organization for their time and support during the audit process. Also, any praise to the audit escorts (if any) can be provided in this statement. This will set the baseline for the next section of the report, in which the audit objective, scope, audit team leader's and auditor's names, dates and places of the audit activities, audit criteria, findings, and conclusions are presented. Each finding must be listed in order of importance (from critical to minor), with the supporting evidence beneath it. The conclusion must state whether the audit objectives were accomplished or not. Other audit evidence which does not support findings may be included in a separate category, as well as any areas not covered within the scope of the audit and any unresolved diverging opinions. An example of an Audit Report template is provided in Appendix D.

Any request for corrective action may appear in the closing remarks of the report, along with the date of the expected response from the auditee's management. Those requests for corrective actions are often presented in a separate, standardized form. An example of a Corrective Action Request form is provided in Appendix D. The audit findings may be addressed singularly or collectively. That is, each finding will be listed individually, or some related findings can be combined into one single finding. The findings must be presented in the audit report using a risk-based approach; that is, critical findings are listed first, then major findings, and finally the minor findings. Each finding must have some form of unique identification, such an alphanumeric code. This code must be used by both the auditors and the auditee to refer to the audit findings during the follow-up stage.

Although there is not any standard format about the required elements in an audit report, there are some items that must not be included in the audit report:

- Any confidential or proprietary information.
- Any subjective opinion.
- Any recommendation, unless required by the auditee's management.
- Minor deficiencies corrected during the audit.
- Generally, more than six or seven findings (try to combine into fewer findings).
- Names of individuals associated with specific findings.
- Any finding not presented during the closing meeting.

If the auditors inadvertently forgot to present any finding during the closing meeting, these omitted findings must be presented to and discussed with the auditee prior to including them in the formal audit report and sent to the audit client. As mentioned before, although all the auditors' signatures are recommended, the audit team leader's signature is imperative; otherwise, the audit report is considered null. The audit process is considered completed, when all the activities described in the audit plan have been carried out and the report has been sent to the audit client. "Completing" the audit must not be confused with "Closing" the audit, which happens after all the corrective action requests have been completed and approved by the audit team.

The audit report and pertinent documents should be retained for a specified time, as required by the audit program, audit authority, or the client. If no time is specified, the records must be kept at least until the next audit. The main reason is that all these records could be used during the planning stage of subsequent audits.

7.2 Writing the Audit Report

After presenting the draft report during the closing meeting, the audit team must focus on the formal audit report that will be sent to the audit client. The report must be sent on a timely manner, usually less than a month after the closing meeting. It must be written in an understandable manner, so it provides independent and objective information that people can act upon. The main problems to avoid when writing the report are poor organization and writing, extraneous information, surprise findings not presented during the closing meeting, unsupported allegations or opinions, and corrective action solutions.

The audit team leader should report the audit conclusions in accordance with the audit program. The audit report should provide a complete, accurate, concise, and clear record of the audit, and should include or refer to the following:

- Audit objectives.
- Audit scope, particularly identification of the organization (the auditee) and the functions or processes audited.
- Identification of the audit client.
- Identification of audit team and auditee's participants in the audit.
- Dates and locations where the audit activities were conducted.
- Audit criteria.
- Audit findings and related evidence.
- Audit conclusions.
- A statement on the degree to which the audit criteria have been fulfilled.
- Any unresolved diverging opinions between the audit team and the auditee.
- Audits by nature are a sampling exercise. As such there is a risk that the audit evidence examined is not representative.

The audit report can also include or refer to the following, as appropriate:

- The audit plan including time schedule.
- A summary of the audit process, including any obstacles encountered that may decrease the reliability of the audit conclusions.

- Confirmation that the audit objectives have been achieved within the audit scope in accordance with the audit plan.
- Any areas within the audit scope not covered including any issues of availability of evidence, resources, or confidentiality, with related justifications.
- A summary covering the audit conclusions and the main audit findings that support them.
- Good practices identified.
- Agreed action plan follow-up, if any.
- A statement of the confidential nature of the contents.
- Any implications for the audit program or subsequent audits.

7.3 Distributing the Audit Report

The audit report should be issued to the audit client within an agreed timeframe. If it is delayed, the reasons should be communicated to the audit client, the auditee, and the individual(s) managing the audit program. The audit report should be dated, reviewed, and accepted, as appropriate, in accordance with the audit program. The audit report should then be distributed to the relevant interested parties defined in the audit program or audit plan. When distributing the audit report, appropriate measures to ensure confidentiality should be considered.

7.4 Completing the Audit

The audit is completed when all planned audit activities have been carried out, or as otherwise agreed with the audit client. Documented information pertaining to the audit should be retained or disposed of by agreement between the participating parties and in accordance with audit program and applicable requirements. Unless required by law, the audit team and the individual(s) managing the audit program should not disclose any information obtained during the audit, or the audit report, to any other party without the explicit approval of the audit client and, where appropriate, the approval of the auditee. If disclosure of the contents of an audit document is required, the audit client and auditee should be informed as soon as possible.

Chapter 8:
Audit Follow-Up

The objective of the follow-up audit is to determine whether the corrective actions were implemented and if they were effective. After the audit report has been submitted to the audit client and distributed to the auditee, it is the responsibility of auditee's upper management to develop and implement a corrective action plan. To accomplish this task, the auditee should have a documented procedure for corrective and preventive actions. Among other things, the procedure should include the assignment of responsibilities, the evaluation of potential importance, the investigation process to identify probable causes, the implementation of corrective and preventive actions, and the evaluation of the effectiveness of these actions. The types of actions expected from the auditee can be classified as:

- **Corrections**: these are the immediate, containment, or remedial actions that address the nonconformance. Because the corrections address the symptoms, not the root causes that produced the nonconformity, these actions fix the problem temporarily but will not avoid the reoccurrence of the failure.
- **Corrective actions**: these actions address the causes of a detected nonconformity to avoid the reoccurrence of the failure. If the permanent corrective actions cannot be implemented immediately, then interim actions need to be implemented. Once the permanent corrective actions are

implemented, the interim actions can be either removed or converted to permanent actions.

- **Preventive actions**: these actions address the causes of a potential nonconformity to avoid the occurrence of the failure. If the permanent preventive actions cannot be implemented immediately, then interim actions need to be implemented. Once the permanent preventive actions are implemented, the interim actions can be either removed or converted to permanent actions.

The corrective and preventive actions, and the subsequent follow-up audits should be completed within a timeframe agreed to by the audit client and the auditees, in consultation with the auditing organization. For first-party audits, the schedule for follow-up audit is normally between two weeks to three months after the completion of the corrective and preventive actions. However, for second-party and third-party audits, the follow-up audits are normally completed within the next audit cycle, which could be from one to three years after the issuance of the corrective action requests.

After the corrective and preventive actions have been implemented, and their effectiveness have been verified, the corrective action request may be considered for closure. The purpose of auditing and issuing corrective action requests is to improve the system. The deficient areas identified during the audit should be re-audited after the completion of the corrective action request. Usually, the audit closure is documented in the corrective action request form. Audit follow-up on corrective actions is one of the weakest links of the audit program.

Chapter 9:
Virtual Audits

Virtual audits are conducted when an organization performs work or provides a service using an online environment allowing persons irrespective of physical locations to execute processes. Auditing of a virtual location is sometimes referred to as virtual auditing. Remote audits refer to using technology to gather information, interview an auditee, when "face-to- face" methods are not possible or desired.

A virtual audit follows the standard audit process while using technology to verify objective evidence. The auditee and audit team should ensure appropriate technology requirements for virtual audits which can include:

- Ensuring the audit team is using agreed remote access protocols, including requested devices, software, and so on.
- Conducting technical checks ahead of the audit to resolve technical issues.
- Ensuring contingency plans are available and communicated including provision for extra audit time if necessary.

Auditor competencies for virtual audits should be the same as for on-site audits. However, for virtual audits, competencies for the auditors should also include:

- Technical skills to use the appropriate electronic equipment and other technology while auditing.

- Experience in facilitating meetings virtually to conduct the audit remotely.

When conducting the opening meeting for virtual audits, the auditor should consider the following aspects:
- Risks associated with virtual or remote audits.
- Using floor plans or diagrams of remote locations for reference, or mapping of electronic information.
- Facilitating for the prevention of background noise disruptions and interruptions.
- Asking for permission in advance to take screenshot copies of documents or any kind of recordings and considering confidentiality and security matters.
- Ensuring confidentiality and privacy during audit breaks. For example, by muting microphones, pausing cameras, and so on.

With the advancements in technology, the virtual audit experience can be very similar to the face-to-face audits. For example, many virtual meetings tools allow the creation of virtual breakout rooms and/or waiting rooms. For example, if there are three auditors in a specific audit, five virtual breakout rooms can be created: one virtual breakout room to be used as the main room, one virtual breakout room for the audit team meetings, and three virtual breakout rooms for the auditors (one for each auditor).

The waiting room can be used to hold attendees outside of the meeting before they are moved to the main room. In the main room, the opening meeting, daily briefings, and closing meetings can be conducted. After the opening meeting, some of the attendees could be sent back to the waiting room and others can be sent to the individual auditor's virtual breakout room for the interview process. Once an individual interview is completed, that person can be dismissed from the meeting and another person brought into the auditor's virtual breakout room. This will continue until all the auditees have been interviewed.

The audit team meeting can be conducted at any time, with only the auditors present and no external interventions. Later, the daily briefing (if necessary) and the closing meeting can be conducted at the main room. Keep in mind that it is better to move attendees from the waiting room to the main room than to always keep attendees in the main room.

Another advantage of virtual meeting's platforms is that they allow to share files electronically within the same platform. In this way, the record-sharing process can be streamlined, and the documents can be shared in real-time. The main disadvantage of virtual audits is that the facility's tour cannot be done physically. However, the audit team leader can request the auditee to provide a video of the facilities to be audited in advance. In this way, the auditor can get acquainted with the process and decide which information will be required during the interview and data collection process.

Chapter 10:
Developing an
Internal Audits Certification

To enhance your internal audits program, it is highly recommended that you certify your auditors. As an example, we are including the Internal Auditing Certification model our company has developed.

9.1. Contents of the certification

The Internal Auditing Certification is a comprehensive certification course with a total duration of three days equivalent to 21 contact hours. Approximately 50% of this time is be devoted to practice exercises. This certification covers the following seven elements:

- Audit basics
- QMS auditor qualifications
- Roles and responsibilities of auditors
- The audit checklist
- Planning and conducting audits
- The closing meeting and audit report
- Audit follow-up and closure

Upon completion of this certification program, participants will be able to:

- Identify the most widely used auditing tools and techniques.

- Apply the appropriate tools for each situation faced on a daily basis by an internal quality auditor.

Our company, Business Excellence Consulting Inc. (BEC), is accredited by the International Association for Continuing Education and Training (IACET). BEC complies with the ANSI/IACET Standard, which is recognized internationally as a standard of excellence in instructional practices. As a result of this accreditation, BEC is authorized to issue the IACET CEU (2.1 CEUs) for this program. Full attendance to the learning event is mandatory to receive CEUs. The detailed content of the certification is described in table 9.1.

Table 9.1: Internal Auditing Certification

Opening Remarks and Pre-Test

Audit Basics
- Audit Stages
- Definitions
- General Types of Audits
- Audit Purpose and Objectives
- Audit Evidence
- Analysis of Audit Nonconformities

QMS Auditor Qualifications
- Qualification Criteria for Auditors
- Maintenance and Improvement of Competence
- Auditor Evaluation

Roles and Responsibilities of Auditors
- Audit Roles and Responsibilities
- Auditor Independence
- Auditor Objectivity

The Audit Checklist
- Purpose of the Audit Checklist
- Requirements of Questions on Audit Checklists
- Contents of the Audit Checklist

Planning and Conducting Audits
- Audit Planning Elements
- Audit Notification
- The Audit Cycle
- Initiating the Audit
- Conducting Document Review
- Conducting On-Site Activities
    - o   The Opening Meeting

Practice Exercise #2
- Preparing for an Opening Meeting

Planning and Conducting Audits (cont.)
- Conducting On-Site Activities
    - o   Communication During the Audit
    - o   Interviews
    - o   Generating Audit Findings
    - o   Preparing Audit Conclusions

Practice Exercise #3
- Audit Interviews and Field Work

Practice Exercise #4
- Post-Audit Preparation

The Closing Meeting and Audit Report
- Conducting the Closing Meeting
- Elements of the Audit Report
- Writing the Audit Report

Practice Exercise #5
- Performing a Closing Meeting

Practice Exercise #6
- Writing the Audit Report

Audit Follow-Up and Closure

Final Exam

M. Peña-Rodríguez

Appendices

Appendix A:
Procedure for Auditor Qualification

1.0 PURPOSE

To define the methodology and requirements applicable to the qualification of auditors for the performance of external audits.

2.0 SCOPE

This procedure applies to ABC's personnel performing audits.

3.0 DEFINITIONS AND ACRONYMS

3.1 ABC: ABC Manufacturing Inc.

3.2 QSM: ABC's Quality System Manager

3.3 Qualified Auditor: a person who fulfils all the requirements set forth in this procedure

3.4 Prospective Auditor: a person who applies as a Qualified Auditor and is participating in the qualification process

3.5 Qualification: the action or fact of becoming qualified as a recognized practitioner of a profession or activity

4.0 PROCEDURE

4.1 List of Qualified Auditors

    4.1.1 The QSM must maintain a List of Qualified Auditors (Form ABC-F-0102-1, Current Revision). This list must be sent to ABCC's President.

    4.1.2 The evidence of the qualification of the auditors must be kept by the QSM and checked by ABC's President, at least annually.

4.2 Auditor Personal Attributes

    4.2.1 Auditors must show the following attributes:

4.2.1.1 Capability to communicate effectively, both in writing and oral, in its native language.

4.2.1.2 Capability to communicate effectively, both in writing and oral, in the language of the audit.

4.2.1.3 Capability to issue the assessment report, at least, in the English language.

4.2.1.4 Professional behavior (exhibiting at the workplace a courteous, conscientious, and generally business-like demeanor).

4.2.1.5 Diplomatic (tactful in dealing with people).

4.2.1.6 Open-minded (willing to consider alternative ideas or points of view).

4.2.1.7 Observant (actively aware of physical surroundings and activities).

4.2.1.8 Self-reliant (acting and functioning autonomously).

4.2.1.9 Organized (exhibiting effective time management, prioritization, planning and efficiency).

4.2.1.10 Decisive (achieving timely decisions based on logical reasoning and analysis).

4.2.1.11 Morally courageous (willing to act responsibly and ethically even though these actions may not always be popular and may sometimes result in disagreement or confrontation).

4.2.2 The behaviors must be evaluated through direct interview by the QSM.

4.2.3 Traceability of the evaluation must be ensured. Refer to Form ABC-F-0102-3, Current Revision (Record of Qualification).

4.2.4 The corresponding records must be kept in auditor's qualification file.

4.3 Auditor Training

4.3.1 Prospective auditors must receive training, to the extent necessary, for assuring auditing competence including:

4.3.1.1 A training in fundamentals for audits, including objectives, organization, documentation, and questioning techniques, and auditing techniques for examining, questioning, evaluating, and reporting, together with methods for identifying and following up corrective actions and closing out audit findings.

4.3.1.2 A training on general structure of quality management systems based on the regulation, normative, and or applicable standard for the audit being performed.

4.3.1.2.1 Examples of trainings to comply with this section are: 21 CFR 211, 21 CFR 820, ISO 9001, ISO 22000, ISO 13485, PIC/S, WHO, ICH Q7, ASQ Certified Quality Auditor Academia, ASQ Certified CGMP Professional Academia, ASQ Certified Biomedical Auditor Academia, ASQ Certified HACCP Academia.

4.3.2 Traceability of the evaluation must be ensured. Refer to Form ABC-F-0102-3, Current Revision (Record of Qualification).

4.3.3 The corresponding records must be kept in auditor's qualification file.

4.4 Initial Qualification Process for Prospective Auditors

4.4.1 The following four (4) criteria must be fulfilled by all prospective auditors:

4.4.1.1 **Criterion #1:** training must have been performed according to Section 4.3.

4.4.1.2 **Criterion #2:** the prospective auditor's education and experience must be evaluated to check if the minimum of 12 credits necessary for getting the qualification can be justified. The scoring system is detailed in Form BEC-F-0102-2, Current Revision (Scoring System).

4.4.1.3 **Criterion #3:** the auditor must have a minimum of five (5) years' work experience in the FDA-regulated industry.

4.4.1.4 **Criterion #4:** the auditor must have participated in a at least one (1) quality management system audit within a period not exceeding three (3) years, prior to the date of qualification.

4.5 Traceability of the evaluation must be ensured. Refer to Form ABC-F-0102-3, Current Revision (Record of Qualification).

4.5.1 The corresponding records must be kept in auditor's qualification file.

4.5.2 Professional certifications, such as ASQ Certified Quality Auditor, ASQ Certified Biomedical Auditor, ASQ Certified HACCP Auditor, ASQ Certified CGMP Professional, ISO 9001, ISO 22000, ISO 13485, and others, are highly desirable.

4.6 Delivery of Qualification

4.6.1 Submission of applications

4.6.1.1 The application must be accompanied by a file containing:

4.6.1.1.1 Applicant's Curriculum Vitae.

4.6.1.1.2 Documents as evidence of pre-requisites.

4.6.1.1.3 Documents as evidence of in-house and/or external training.

4.6.1.1.4 If necessary, additional documents as evidence of the applicant's work experience.

4.6.1.2 Documents are filed by the QSM and archived for 10 years.

4.6.2 Issuance of qualification

4.6.2.1 The application must be reviewed and approved by the QSM.

4.7 Maintenance of Proficiency

4.7.1 To maintain his/her proficiency, the auditor must have at least:

4.7.1.1 Participated in three (3) audits in the last three (3) years with a minimum of nine (9) audit days.

4.7.1.2 Reviewed and studied codes, standards, procedures, instructions, and other documents related to quality management systems.

4.7.1.3 Participated in continuous education program with a minimum of 21 contact hours.

4.8 Renewal of Qualification

4.8.1 Qualifications are valid during three (3) years.

4.8.2 The request for renewal of qualification must contain at least:

4.8.2.1 Report of services (date, duration, technical field, position during the audit, approximate size of organization audited) performed by the auditor within the framework of the qualification.

4.8.2.2 Documents as evidence of attendance at any training and informational courses.

4.9 Withdrawal of Qualification

4.9.1 The qualification may be withdrawn or suspended at any time:

4.9.1.1 In case of no assessment activity during the certification period.

4.9.1.2 After a non-satisfactory supervision and/or examination of an audit report.

4.9.1.3 Following a client's significant claim.

4.9.1.4 Following any other relevant information or event.

4.9.1.5 Upon request of the auditor's management.

4.9.2 In addition, any auditor who no longer performs assessments for ABC (because of transfer, departure from the company, or other reason) forfeits his/her qualification.

4.10 Monitoring of Auditors

4.10.1 During the period of validity of the qualification, monitoring of auditor is carried out by his/her local management. Monitoring includes at least:

4.10.1.1 Evaluation of minimum activity.

4.10.1.2 Report supervision.

4.10.1.3 Examination of any relevant document (e.g., external claim or internal audit report).

4.10.2 Any lack of monitoring will automatically lead to the loss of the qualification at the end of the qualification period.

5.0   RELATED DOCUMENTS

5.1 Form ABC-F-0102-1, Current Revision (List of Qualified Auditors)

5.2 Form ABC-F-0102-2, Current Revision (Scoring System)

5.3 Form ABC-F-0102-3, Current Revision (Record of Qualification)

6.0   REVISION HISTORY

Revision Level	Revision Date	Revision Comment
A	08/16/21	Original Issuance.

7.0 APPROVALS

Written By: _____   Date: _____
                Quality Systems Manager

Approved By: _____   Date: _____
                    President

74

Appendix B:
Record of Auditor Qualification

Prospective Auditor's Name:_____

Qualification Requirements

	Evaluated By:	Position:		Date:
Evaluation of Personal Behaviors				

	Contents	Date(s)	Duration (Hrs.)	Trainer
Training Courses	Auditing Fundamentals			
	Current Good Manufacturing Practices or Quality System Regulation			
	Other (specify):			
	Other (specify):			

Education	Maximum Degree Achieved	Number of Credits (non-cumulative. Maximum 6 credits)
	Areas of Expertise	Number of Credits (Cumulative)
	Technical experience in engineering, lifesciences, or quality assurance	
Work Experience	2 or more years in FDA-regulated industry	
	2 or more years in quality assurance	
	2 or more in auditing quality assurance systems	
	Certification Title(s)	Number of Credits
Professional Certifications		
Total Number of Credits (minimum of 12 credits are required)		

	Company Audited	Type of Audit / Duration	Date(s)
Auditing Experience			

For ABC Manufacturing Inc. use only:

Result of Qualification:	☐Approved ☐Not Approved Reason:
QSM Signature:	Date:

Appendix C:
Scoring System for the Record of Auditor Qualification

Education

Number of Credits (Non-cumulative; maximum of 6 credits)	Education Level
4 credits	Technical degree in engineering, lifesciences, or quality assurance from an accredited institution in the country of origin.
5 credits	License / Bachelor's degree (or equivalent) in engineering, lifesciences, or quality assurance from an accredited institution in the country of origin.
6 credits	Master's degree (or equivalent) in engineering, lifesciences, or quality assurance from an accredited institution in the country of origin.

Work Experience

Number of Credits (Cumulative)	Education Level
1 credit for each full year, with a maximum of 5 credits for this aspect of experience	Technical experience in engineering, lifesciences, or quality assurance.
1 credit	If 2 or more years of this experience have been in the FDA-regulated industry.
2 credits	If 2 or more years of this experience have been in quality assurance.
3 credits	If 2 or more years of this experience have been in auditing quality assurance systems

Professional Certifications

Number of Credits (Cumulative; maximum of 5 credits)	Certification
1 credit for each certification	ASQ Certified Quality Auditor, ASQ Certified Biomedical Auditor, ASQ Certified HACCP Auditor, ASQ Certified CGMP Professional, ISO 9001, ISO 22000, ISO 13485, RAB Lead Auditor, and so on.

Appendix D:
Audit Report Templates

INTERNAL REVIEW REPORT

Lead Auditor:	Date:	Page ____ of ____

Audit objectives and scope:

Audit plan, criteria, and references:

Audit team members:

Executive summary:

INTERNAL REVIEW REPORT

Lead Auditor:	Date:	Page ____ of ____

Audit findings:

INTERNAL REVIEW REPORT

Lead Auditor:	Date:	
		Page ____ of ____

Observations / Comments:

Audit report distribution list:

Audit conclusions:

☐ NO corrective actions requested ☐ Corrective actions requested
☐ Follow-Up Required ☐ Follow-Up Not Required

Lead Auditor's Approval:	Date:

CORRECTIVE ACTION REQUEST

Initiator:	Date:	Type of Action Requested: ☐ Corrective ☐ Preventive

TO BE COMPLETED BY AUDITOR
Description of nonconformity (include as appropriate: what, when, where, how, and who)
21 CFR 211 Requirement:

TO BE COMPLETED BY AUDITEE
Results of investigation:
Actions to be taken:

TO BE COMPLETED BY AUDITOR	
Verification:	
☐ Satisfactory	☐ Unsatisfactory
☐ Follow-Up Required	☐ Follow-Up Not Required
Verified by:	Verification Date:

I

84

Appendix E:
Practice Exercises

Practice Exercise #1: Writing good checklist requirements

1. Form into groups.
2. Work with your group to analyze one of the assigned procedures.
3. Develop a checklist that would guide an effective audit interview for your assigned procedure.
4. This checklist should enable an auditor to identify evidence of conformity or nonconformity.
5. Requirements on the checklists may be supplemented with audit questions.
6. Present your answers to the class.

Practice Exercise #2: Preparing for an Opening Meeting

1. Form into groups.
2. Work with your team to discuss how would you conduct an Opening Meeting.
3. Refer to the "Checklist for Evaluating Opening Meetings" presented in the material.
4. As you review the checklist, briefly discuss how will you conduct the Opening Meeting.
5. During the Opening Meeting, you will need to role play or improvise in order to conduct the "simulated" Opening Meeting exercise.

Practice Exercise #3: Audit Interviews and Field Work

1. Form into the assigned audit teams.
2. Using the checklist developed earlier, interview the appropriate personnel to complete the performance phase of the audit.
3. Use the interview techniques learned in this section.

Practice Exercise #4: Post-Audit Preparation

1. Once the interviews are completed, meet with your audit team to reach consensus about the observations and findings.
2. Determine the information each auditor will be presenting for the closing meeting.

Practice Exercise #5: Performing a Closing Meeting

1. Form into the assigned audit teams.
2. Using the information obtained during the planning and performance phases of the audit, prepare a brief MS PowerPoint presentation for the Closing Meeting.
3. During the Closing Meeting, you will need to role play or improvise to conduct the "simulated" Closing Meeting exercise.

Practice Exercise #6: Writing the Audit Report

1. Using the templates provided, prepare the Audit Report.

Bibliography

FDA. *21 Code od Federal Regulation Part 820: Medical Devices: Current Good Manufacturing Practice (CGMP) Final Rule: Quality System Regulations* (1996). Can be downloaded from: http://www.ecfr.gov.

FDA. *21 Code of Federal Regulation Part 211: Current Good Manufacturing Practice (CGMP) for Finished Pharmaceuticals* (1978). Can be downloaded from: http://www.ecfr.gov.

FDA. *Guidance for Industry: ICH Q10 Pharmaceutical Quality System* (2009).

International Standard, ISO 19011:2018 *Guidelines for Auditing Management Systems*

José Rodríguez-Pérez, *Handbook of Investigation and Effective CAPA Systems*, (Milwaukee: ASQ Quality Press, 2016).

About the Author

Manuel E. Peña Rodríguez is a process improvement and training consultant with more than 25 years of experience in many industry sectors. Since January 2006, he is fully devoted to consulting under Business Excellence Consulting Inc. He also served as professor in the graduate program in biochemistry at the University of Puerto Rico, Medical Sciences Campus, in San Juan PR. Mr. Peña Rodríguez received his Juris Doctor degree from the Pontifical Catholic University of Puerto Rico and his Master of Engineering in Engineering Management degree from Cornell University in Ithaca NY.

He is also a licensed Professional Engineer registered in Puerto Rico and an attorney registered in the Supreme Court of Puerto Rico and the U.S. District Court for the District of Puerto Rico. Mr. Peña Rodríguez is an ASQ Certified Six Sigma Black Belt, Manager of Quality & Organizational Excellence, Quality Engineer, Quality Auditor, Biomedical Auditor, and HACCP Auditor. He is also a Senior member of ASQ and former Chair of the Puerto Rico ASQ Section.

Mr. Peña Rodríguez is the author of the books "Statistical Process Control for the FDA- Regulated Industry" and "Process Monitoring and Improvement Handbook", published by ASQ Quality Press. Mr. Peña Rodríguez is also the author of the article "Serious About Samples: Understanding Different Approaches for Process Monitoring and When to Use Them" and co-author (with José Rodríguez-Pérez) of the articles "Fail- Safe FMEA", "CAPA Pitfalls and Pratfalls", and "Essential Evaluation". All those articles were published in the monthly editions of the ASQ Quality Progress magazine.

He can be reached at manuel@calidadpr.com.

Index

Made in the USA
Middletown, DE
18 January 2022